ARCHBISHOP DESMOND TUTU
and DOUGLAS CARLTON ABRAMS

GOD'S DREAM

illustrated by LEUYEN PHAM

WALKER BOOKS
AND SUBSIDIARIES
LONDON · BOSTON · SYDNEY · AUCKLAND

Dear child of God,
What do you dream of
in your loveliest dreams?

Do you dream of a rainbow
reaching across the sky?

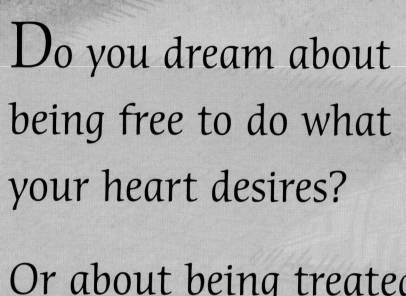

Do you dream about being free to do what your heart desires?

Or about being treated like a full person no matter how young you might be?

Do you know what God dreams of?

Close your eyes and look with your heart, dear child...

God dreams about people sharing.

God dreams about people caring.

God dreams that we reach out and hold one another's hands and play one another's games and laugh with one another's hearts.

But God does not force us to be friends or to love one another...

Dear child of God, it does happen
that we get angry and hurt one another.
Then we feel sad and very alone.
Sometimes we cry, and God cries with us...

But when we say we're sorry
and forgive one another,
we wipe away our tears and
God's tears too.

Each of us carries a piece
of God's heart within us.

And when we love one another, the pieces of God's heart are made whole.

God dreams that every one of us will see that we are all brothers and sisters — yes, even you and me — even if we have different mummies and daddies or live in different faraway lands...

Even if we speak different languages
or have different ways of talking to God.
Even if we have different eyes or
different skin...

Even if you
are taller and
I am smaller.

Even if your nose is little
and mine is large.

Dear child of God, do you know how to make God's dream come true? It is really quite easy.

As easy as sharing, loving, caring.
As easy as holding, playing, laughing.

As easy as knowing we are one big family because we are all God's children. Will you help God's dream come true?

Let me tell you a secret...

God smiles like a
rainbow when you do.

For our children and grandchildren and for all people
-young and old-
who help God's dream come true.
D. T. & D. C. A.

For my own little dream, Leo
L. P.

First published 2008 by Walker Books Ltd
87 Vauxhall Walk, London SE11 5HJ

2 4 6 8 10 9 7 5 3 1

Text © 2008 Archbishop Desmond Tutu and Douglas Carlton Abrams
Illustrations © 2008 LeUyen Pham

The right of Archbishop Desmond Tutu and Douglas Carlton Abrams and LeUyen Pham
to be identified as authors and illustrator respectively of this work
has been asserted by them in accordance with the Copyright, Designs and Patents Act 1988

This book has been typeset in ITC Cerigo Book.

Printed in China

British Library Cataloguing in Publication Data:
a catalogue record for this book is available from the British Library

ISBN 978-1-4063-1819-7

www.walkerbooks.co.uk

ARCHBISHOP DESMOND TUTU

was awarded the Nobel Peace Prize in 1984 for his lifelong struggle to bring equality, justice and peace to his native South Africa. Between 1986 and 1996, he served as Archbishop of Cape Town. In 1995, former South African President Nelson Mandela asked him to lead the Truth and Reconciliation Commission, which became a model of national forgiveness and coexistence. Archbishop Tutu is currently Chairperson of the Elders, an international group of world leaders, peace activists and human rights advocates charged with helping to end conflicts and solve global problems (www.TheElders.org). His most recent book is *God Has a Dream: A Vision of Hope for Our Time.* He continues to play an important role worldwide as a spokesperson for peace and forgiveness. Archbishop Tutu lives in South Africa with his wife, Leah. They have four children and seven grandchildren.

DOUGLAS CARLTON ABRAMS

is the coauthor with Archbishop Desmond Tutu of *God Has a Dream: A Vision of Hope for Our Time.* His many books have been translated into more than two dozen languages. He is the cofounder of Idea Architects, a book and media development agency working with visionary authors to create a wiser, healthier and more just world. Douglas Carlton Abrams lives in California with his wife and their three children.

LeUyen Pham

is the author-illustrator of *Big Sister, Little Sister* and has illustrated many other books for children, including *Freckleface Strawberry* by Julianne Moore. About *God's Dream*, LeUyen Pham says, "Being a part of this book, which has such a peaceful message, has been an extremely significant experience for me, considering that I left war-torn Vietnam during the fall of Saigon when I was only a year old. My son was also born during the creation of this book, bringing the lovely message of hope and love full circle." LeUyen Pham lives and works in San Francisco with her husband and son.